The Battle Within

By

Cynthia Mandel

Copyright

Copyright © 2025 Cynthia Mandel

Published by

All rights reserved. No part of this book may be reproduced or transmitted in any form or by any means, electronic or mechanical, including photocopying, recording, or by any information storage and retrieval system, without written permission from the publisher and author.

Foreword

Two thumbs, talk-to-text, and running through an airport—that's my friend, Cynthia Mandel! She's fire and motion, vulnerability and strength, grit and grace. I've had the privilege of walking alongside Cynthia in our Mastermind Group for the past three years, and I can tell you she's the real deal!

Cynthia's inspirational journey began in deep emotional pain. A wounded little girl turned to food to survive what she couldn't understand or explain. She never felt worthy of love, never fully believed she was enough to be chosen, seen, or even safe. And yet, here she is—offering up her story, not for sympathy, but for our breakthrough.

This book reveals many of her traumatic soul scars in a way that few dare to. The Battle Within is not just a story of weight loss—it's a story of life reclamation. Cynthia lost more than 200 pounds, yes—but she also shed her shame and the belief that she was too broken to ever heal.

As you read her story, you'll certainly recognize parts of your own. Maybe the circumstances are different, but the emotions—the heartache, the anger, the feeling of abandonment—they live in the same places in all of us. And that's what makes Cynthia's vulnerability so powerful. It gives us permission to finally stop hiding. It invites us to tell the truth about our own pain.

I'm so grateful Cynthia is courageous enough to go first—because in doing so, she leads the way for so many others. Her voice doesn't whine about what she's been through—it boldly declares, "If I can do it, you can too!" That kind of hope is rare. That kind of inspiration is contagious. And that kind of woman? She's an absolute gift!

THE BATTLE WITHIN
by Cynthia Mandel

Take a deep breath. Open your heart and let her story speak to yours. And get ready... because your battle within is not the end—it's the beginning of your victory!

— Nicole Crank

Television Host, Author, Speaker, Mentor Lead Co-Pastor of FaithChurch.com

Dedication

For the broken, the hurting, and the ones who feel forgotten—for every survivor still fighting their battle within—may these pages remind you that your story isn't over, that healing is possible, and freedom is real.

Acknowledgement

This book was born out of scars, tears, and the relentless pull of a God who refused to let me go. To everyone who showed up for me in the moments when I wanted to quit—you know who you are. Your belief in me when I had nothing left gave me the strength to keep turning pain into purpose.

To my publisher and the team who worked tirelessly to shape this manuscript into something that could be held in another's hands—thank you for seeing the story beneath the brokenness and helping me bring it to life. To the doctors, nurses, and trainers who poured into me—you weren't just treating a body; you were helping rebuild a soul.

To Pastors David and Nicole Crank—you changed my life in ways words will never fully capture. You gave me hope and love that I had never known before, and through your ministry I learned that God truly does write beauty from ashes.

To Don Strange, thank you in a special way. Your impact on my journey cannot be measured in simple words—you showed me what strength, discipline, and belief could do when poured into someone who had nearly given up.

Most of all, I want to thank God. Every page of this book is proof that He never abandoned me, not in the darkest pit, not in the loneliest night. His grace carried me, His love restored me, and His purpose gave me the courage to keep breathing when I didn't want to anymore.

Finally, to every reader holding this book—you are the reason I kept writing. This story is not just mine; it's ours. If these words give you even a spark of hope, then every battle I've fought was worth it.

THE BATTLE WITHIN
by Cynthia Mandel

Table of Contents

INTRODUCTION 8
CHAPTER 1: THE BREAKING POINT 10
CHAPTER 2: SUGARCOATED PAIN 17
CHAPTER 3: BREAKING FREE: HOW I LOST 253 POUNDS .. 26
CHAPTER 4: CHANGE STARTS FROM WITHIN 33
CHAPTER 5: SURVIVING AGAINST THE ODDS 40
CHAPTER 6: IDENTIFYING EMOTIONAL TRIGGERS 46
CHAPTER 7: REWRITING THE STORY: OVERCOMING LIMITING BELIEFS 55
CHAPTER 8: SPOTLIGHT: DON STRANGE — THE TRAINER BEHIND THE REAL CHANGE 62
CHAPTER 9: LIVING IN THE FREEDOM YOU FOUGHT FOR 67
CHAPTER 10 : YOUR NEXT S.T.E.P. 72
DON'S TRAINING PHILOSOPHY 80

INTRODUCTION

I know how it feels to be trapped in a body that doesn't reflect who you truly are inside. I know the frustrations of trying every diet under the sun only to fall back into old, destructive habits. I know the pain of feeling invisible in an aesthetically-driven world that often judges us by our size.

But I also know what it feels like to find the courage to take control to break free from the vicious, self-harming, addictive cycle, and to finally believe that change is possible and that I am enough.

If I can lose 253 pounds, so can you! No matter the amount, it's within your reach.

That's not just a motivational slogan – it's the truth.

Food was my comfort, escape, and best friend for most of my life. I did not just struggle with my weight; I struggled with why I was eating in the first place. My self-identity as intrinsically linked to food!

My journey to losing over 250 pounds wasn't just about cutting calories or finding the 'right' diet – it was about completely transforming my relationship with food.

This book isn't about a quick fix. It is not about a fad diet or a trendy healing from the inside out. IT is about uncovering why we turn to food for comfort and learning how to take back control – reclaiming the driver's seat in our own lives and navigating our desired destination.

In these pages, I'll take you through my life journey – the struggles, the setbacks, and the triumphs. I'll share the reasons I weighed so much, the emotional wounds that led me to seek comfort and company in food, and the turning points that helped me finally regain control.

More importantly, I'll empower you with the tools that helped me get there. The daily habits. The proven strategies that did not just help me lose weight – but keep it off for good.

I want you to know that you are not alone. Whatever has been holding you back – whether it is emotional eating, fear, self-doubt, loneliness, or a past that still haunts you – you have the power to change. I am living proof of that.

So, if you have ever felt stuck, hopeless, or convinced you could never lose weight and transform your life, I am here to tell you that you absolutely can. And I will show you how, hand in hand step by step. My mission is to offer solutions, not judgement.

I believe in change. I believe in you!

Are you ready?

Let's begin….

CHAPTER 1:
THE BREAKING POINT

It's hard for me to pinpoint exactly when my problems with food began. But when I trace the line backward, it leads to one heartbreaking truth:

My mother died when I was just two years old.

I was a toddler—barely old enough to understand the world around me, let alone the concept of death. But her absence created a silence so deep that I could feel it in my bones. A mother's love is supposed to be a child's first safe harbor... but I never even got to anchor there.

My father loved my mother so deeply that he completely unraveled when she passed. He had a nervous breakdown and had to be hospitalized. And just like that, I lost *both* of my parents—one to death, and the other to a mind that couldn't survive the loss.

I didn't know then what was happening. All I knew was that I was suddenly unwanted, unprotected, and alone. At two years old, I was already being formed by the belief that love could disappear in an instant... and when it did, no one would come to save me.

After that, my father couldn't—or wouldn't—look at me.

He said I looked too much like my mother. That I gave him nightmares. And so, instead of holding onto me, he pushed me away.

He sent me and my older sister to live with our grandparents, who were just around the corner. But it didn't feel like "family." It felt like exile. I didn't know then that my father had been institutionalized. I didn't understand the full weight of what had happened until I was seventeen years old. Until then, I just thought I was being rejected—again.

My grandmother, Rose, was a high-class woman. She was a respected decorator and ran an antique shop down the block. Always busy. Always working. Her world was elegant, polished, and scheduled. There was no time—or emotional bandwidth—for little girls grieving in silence.

We were supposed to be watched by the housekeeper. But the truth? We had the run of the building. And **that freedom cost me everything**.

I was six years old the first time it happened.

His name was Aleisio. He was the doorman—the person trusted to watch over the residents, to protect us. Instead, he preyed on me.

He would lead me into closets or storage rooms and violate my innocence in the most terrifying ways. I didn't understand what was happening—I was just a child—but I knew it felt wrong. I knew it made me feel dirty, confused, and afraid.

Afterward, he would hand me a quarter.

And I would take that quarter, walk down to the corner store, and buy candy.

It sounds like such a small detail—something trivial. But that pattern laid the foundation for a lifetime of pain.

I didn't realize it then, but I was already learning to use food as a way to numb what I didn't have words for.

The candy helped me forget. At least until the next time.

Food became my first best friend.

The first thing that didn't ask questions. Didn't touch me. Didn't make me feel worthless.

Each bite of chocolate, each candy bar, each moment of chewing—it gave me a momentary escape. And that's all I wanted: to escape.

I didn't scream. I didn't fight back. I just ate.

Because in my world, food was the only thing that didn't hurt me.

School was a disaster. I was angry, volatile, and full of rage I

THE BATTLE WITHIN
by Cynthia Mandel

couldn't name.

I fought with everyone—teachers, classmates, anyone who got too close. I was acting out what was happening on the inside. I didn't know how to process the betrayal, the abandonment, the abuse—so I became a walking explosion.

When the school called, Grandma wouldn't come. She always sent the housekeeper. She was too busy. Too refined to deal with broken children.

But every time I got sent home, I got a reward: food.

There was a little diner down the block, and I could order anything I wanted. Hamburgers, pizza with extra cheese and pepperoni, milkshakes, French fries, cookies, and soda. It didn't matter what it cost—I was told to charge it to my grandmother's account.

That food became more than just a meal. It became a *language*. My way of saying, "I'm hurting."

My way of screaming, "Why didn't anybody protect me?"

My way of coping, because no one ever taught me another one.

Looking back now, I can see how food filled in all the gaps. When I couldn't cry, food held me.

When I couldn't talk, food listened.

When I couldn't make sense of the pain, food dulled the noise. But that love came with a cost.

Every pound I gained became a wall—a way to shield myself from further pain. I believed if I was big enough, maybe people would leave me alone. Maybe I could disappear behind the size. Maybe I could be safe.

But inside? I was still that little girl, standing alone in a hallway, with candy in her hand and a wound in her soul.

Things got worse when my father remarried.

Suddenly, I was sent to live with him and my new stepmother,

Helen. I guess he thought we could be a "normal" family. But we weren't. We weren't even close.

They didn't love me. They didn't want me there. And food? Food became a battleground.

They counted the cookies. They marked the milk carton with a Sharpie to track the level. Every bite I took was monitored. Questioned. Criticized.

So I learned to sneak.

I became a cookie thief. A quiet snacker. I waited until no one was looking. I hid wrappers in drawers and under the bed. I learned how to eat without getting caught—and how to hate myself while doing it.

It was never about hunger. It was about *control*.

Because when the world around you makes you feel powerless, food becomes your only form of rebellion.

That's why I say my battle didn't begin with a diet—it began with pain. It began the moment I realized food was safer than people.

This is the truth behind emotional eating.

It's not about greed. It's not about laziness. It's about trauma. And it's time we talk about it.

✱ *Reflection: Where It All Began*

Think back to your earliest memories of comfort. Was food a part of it?

Did you ever feel like eating helped you escape something you couldn't deal with?

You're not alone. You're not broken.

You're just human—and maybe you never had anyone help you understand what you were really hungry for.

_____

_____

_____

_____

_____

_____

_____

_____

_____

_____

_____

_____

_____

_____

_____

Journal Prompts:

- What's your earliest memory of using food to feel better?
- Who or what hurt you before you ever picked up your first diet plan?
- Are there certain foods that feel "safe" or "comforting" for you? Why?

THE BATTLE WITHIN
by Cynthia Mandel

CHAPTER 2:
SUGARCOATED PAIN

Food was never just food. It was shame.

It was punishment. It was survival.

I didn't grow up in a home where meals were shared with laughter or love. In my house, food was a weapon. And if you broke the rules—rules that changed depending on moods— you paid for it. Not with a timeout or a lecture, but with bruises... and a bowl of dry dog food.

Yes. Dog food.

If I did something "wrong"—like eating without permission, or taking something small like a snack—I'd be beaten with a baton. Then, for dinner, I'd be forced to sit and eat dry kibble.

Sometimes, they'd get creative and top it off with a dog biscuit for dessert. It was meant to humiliate me, and it worked. That kind of treatment doesn't just wound your body—it scars your soul.

There's something deeply disturbing about growing up believing that food is a privilege you don't deserve. That nourishment is a reward you earn by being silent, compliant, and invisible.

That's how early it began—my complicated, toxic relationship with food.

It's hard to explain the damage that does to a child. To sit at a table where everyone else is eating a meal and be handed a bowl meant for an animal—because you weren't "good enough" that day.

I didn't know how to name the feeling then, but I do now:

Dehumanized.

I felt subhuman. Like I didn't matter. Like I wasn't worth feeding.

That experience planted a belief in me that would take decades to unlearn:

THE BATTLE WITHIN
by Cynthia Mandel

You don't deserve love. You don't even deserve dinner.

So when people ask me how I gained so much weight, I want to tell them, "Let's go back to that table. The one where I learned I was worthless."

Eventually, my behavior became too much for my father to handle—at least that's what he told himself. But the truth is, I was a little girl acting out the only way I knew how. I was trying to make sense of the trauma, the grief, the instability... the punishment.

Instead of helping me, he gave up.

He packed my things, dropped me off at a residential facility for emotionally disturbed children, and told me not to call. Not to write. Not to reach out.

"If there's something I need to know, the director will call," he said.

That was the beginning of years spent in institutions—three in total—each one deepening the sense that I was unwanted, unfixable, and unworthy of love.

Pleasantville was my first institution. And just like the name, it was a lie.

There was nothing pleasant about it. The walls were cold, the structure was rigid, and the people there—even those who meant well—felt distant. I was required to meet with a therapist twice a week. But I didn't talk. I didn't trust. I had already learned that adults were not safe.

So I sat there with my arms crossed, angry, bitter, and guarded. They wanted to help, maybe. But I wasn't open.

Because the truth was, **I had already given up on being helped.**

The only thing I looked forward to was dessert.

It sounds small, but those cake slices were the highlight of my week. It wasn't about sugar—it was about the ten minutes where I felt like I had something good. I wasn't eating because I was hungry. I was eating because it was the only time I didn't feel forgotten.

THE BATTLE WITHIN
by Cynthia Mandel

By the time I left Pleasantville, I was ten and a half years old... and already 225 pounds.

My next placement was Sagamore. I got smarter there. Not emotionally healthier—but sneakier.

I figured out how to manipulate the system. I offered to help feed the younger kids who couldn't eat by themselves—not out of kindness, but because I knew I could steal their desserts. And I did.

Every time I got the chance, I'd eat in secret, hide the wrappers, and cover my tracks. Food was no longer just comfort. It was power. It was rebellion. It was something I could control in a world where I had no control at all.

I gained 35 pounds in six months. No one questioned it. No one asked me why I was eating so much. No one saw the little girl trying to soothe a wound no one would acknowledge.

At my final institution, Hawthorn, the details blur.

Sometimes I think I blocked the memories out on purpose. But I do remember the cake. They used to bring one to our cottage every few days—meant to be shared between eighteen girls. But I would sneak into the kitchen and eat most of it myself.

It wasn't about gluttony. It was about *desperation*.

Desperation to feel something that didn't hurt. Desperation to prove to myself that I mattered enough to take up space. Desperation to not feel invisible—even if it meant hiding and eating in the dark.

Twice a year, they'd take us shopping for clothes. But because of my size, I couldn't shop with the others. I had to go to a special store—what we called the "old fat ladies' store." I hated it. Every shopping trip reminded me of everything I believed about myself:

- I was too big.
- I was too broken.
- I was never going to be wanted.

Those feelings stayed with me into adulthood. So when I met a man who accepted me— who didn't seem to care about my size—I clung to that. I married the first man who made me feel seen.

He never criticized my weight. But our relationship was far from healthy. He had anger issues. Couldn't keep a job. I became the provider.

And together, we built a life filled with food, chaos, and emotional avoidance.

We always had snacks—Oreos, donuts, ice cream. I had secret stashes everywhere.

Candy in my purse. Cookies under the bed. Twizzlers in the glove box.

I'd eat whole bags of Pepperidge Farm cookies on the way home and toss the evidence before walking through the door.

I made sure dessert was always covered if we were invited somewhere. I couldn't risk showing up and not having something sweet. That panic—the fear of not having sugar—was real. Because sugar wasn't just a craving… it was a *coping mechanism*.

I had created a world where food felt like the only thing I could rely on. And it was killing me.

By 2003, I was 43 years old. And I weighed 430 pounds.

That's when I decided to get gastric bypass surgery.

And physically—it worked. I dropped 250 pounds. I went from 430 to 180 in just over a year. But emotionally? I was still carrying the same weight.

You can lose the size and still live in shame.

You can shrink your body and still be imprisoned in your soul.

When my husband left me, it shattered me. I never saw it coming. He accepted me at my heaviest, but somewhere along the way, something changed. And just like that—he was gone.

It wasn't just a divorce. It was a reminder of every abandonment

I'd ever experienced. "You're not enough."

"You're too much."

"You're not worth staying for." That's what it felt like.

The weight loss had given me a new body, but it couldn't fix what was broken inside.

That's when I realized: **healing isn't about the number on the scale.**

It's about finding the courage to sit with your pain instead of feeding it. It's about learning to comfort yourself with truth instead of sugar.

It's about rewriting the story you were handed and choosing to believe you are worthy— even if no one else ever told you so.

This book is my attempt to help others do the same.

To find freedom not just from food, but from everything that drove you to it in the first place.

You're not weak. You're not broken. You're *surviving*.

And now? You're about to start *living*.

Reflection: Healing the Relationship with Food

Emotional eating is never just about hunger—it's about history.

Journal Prompts:

- What painful memories are tied to food in your life?
- When you think about "comfort foods," what emotions do they actually represent?
- How can you begin to give yourself comfort in *non-food* ways?
- Have you ever used food to fill a need that had nothing to do with nourishment?

THE BATTLE WITHIN
by Cynthia Mandel

Try This:

For one week, keep a "craving journal." Every time you feel the urge to eat something sweet or heavy, pause and ask:

- What just happened?
- What am I really feeling?
- What do I need that food can't give me?

Even if you still eat—just *notice*. Awareness is where freedom begins.

CHAPTER 3:
BREAKING FREE: HOW I LOST 253 POUNDS

Surviving an abusive childhood, being shuffled from institution to institution, enduring multiple suicide attempts, and growing up never feeling truly loved or valued—it's no wonder food became my only joy. Food wasn't just fuel; it was my comfort, my escape, my most loyal companion in a world that had shown me little mercy.

After a devastating divorce, I spiraled into a place I swore I'd never go back to. The pain was unbearable. It felt like I had been abandoned all over again—not just by my partner, but by life itself. Every part of me was screaming for something to hold on to, and I reached for the only thing that had ever offered consistent relief: food.

My days blurred into a fog of surviving—working just enough to get through the day, then going home, eating until I couldn't feel anymore, crying myself to sleep, and waking up to repeat it all over again. It was my own personal version of Groundhog Day, only darker and lonelier. The grief cracked open wounds I thought I had buried. Wounds that whispered lies like: *You're unlovable. You're too far gone. You'll never get better.*

I remember one night in particular. I was on the kitchen floor, clutching a sleeve of cookies, tears streaming down my cheeks. The television buzzed in the background, some rerun I wasn't watching. I whispered through sobs, "What's wrong with me?" It wasn't hunger—I just didn't want to feel anything at all.

Every bite became a sedative—numbing, but never healing. I wasn't eating because I was hungry. I was eating because I was broken. Because I didn't know how else to survive the ache in my soul. My body ballooned with the weight of every painful memory, every unresolved trauma, and every unspoken cry for help.

Even after undergoing gastric bypass surgery, I regained 150 pounds within a year. I clung to that weight like it was armor. It wasn't that the surgery had failed—it's that it had never touched the real issue. The weight wasn't just on my body. It was in my heart. It was in my story. And until I dealt with *that* weight, no surgery in the world could set me free.

Then—something miraculous happened. At 54 years old, this little Jewish girl walked into Faith Church for the first time... and met Jesus.

Or maybe He met me.

Either way, that moment marked the beginning of everything changing.

At first, I didn't walk in with faith—I walked in with desperation. I stood in the back, arms folded tightly around my chest like armor. But as the worship began and the presence of God filled the room, something inside me broke. The worship team sang *Way Maker*, and I could barely stand. The lyrics hit something deep in my soul: *"You are here, healing every heart..."* And for the first time in my life, I thought—what if He really could heal mine?

I cried so hard I thought I'd never stop. But it wasn't the hopeless cry of despair—it was the release of a lifetime of pain. In that moment, I wasn't alone. I was held. And I knew something had shifted.

I started to believe—hesitantly at first—that maybe my life was worth fighting for. That maybe, just maybe, I wasn't too far gone. That maybe God hadn't given up on me, even if I had.

That shift didn't happen overnight. Healing never does. But little by little, I began to try again.

I began with what I could do. I started to eat with more intention and self-respect, losing about 30 pounds on my own. But I quickly realized: I needed help. Real, loving, accountable help.

Spotlight: Don Strange — The Trainer Behind the Transformation
Hi, I'm Don Strange.

At my lowest point, I didn't just need a trainer — I needed someone who could see past the number on the scale and into the battle inside my heart. When I met Don Strange, I found exactly that. He didn't promise me a quick fix. He promised me truth, structure, and the belief

THE BATTLE WITHIN
by Cynthia Mandel

that I could do this. I'll share his story later, but meeting him marked the start of a whole new chapter in my own.

One of the first things Don ever told me was that what you put into your mind is even more important than what you put into your body. That line stuck with me, because at the time my head was full of doubt and fear. He also reminded me that change isn't about what you do once — it's about what you do over and over again, even on the days you don't feel like it. Those ideas planted a seed I didn't know would grow into the transformation you'll read about later.

One Sunday, Pastor David introduced a Connect Group focused on fitness and nutrition. He brought his personal trainer, Don Strange, on stage to speak. Don wasn't just a fitness expert—he was a man of God. As he spoke, something stirred inside me. It was that small, familiar whisper again—the one I was finally learning to recognize as God's voice: *That's your next step.*

So I joined the group. Then I reached out to Don personally. I didn't just need a trainer—I needed someone who understood the war going on inside me. I asked what it would take to work with him one-on-one, and that decision changed the entire trajectory of my life.

Don didn't just work on my body—he helped me see myself through God's eyes. He didn't hand me a diet. He handed me tools. He asked real questions like, "What are you actually willing to commit to?" Not what sounded good. Not what I *hoped* I'd do. What I'd *actually* do—day in and day out, no matter how I felt.

I told him, "I've failed so many times, I don't trust myself."

He looked me dead in the eye and said, "You don't trust yourself... but you hired me. So trust *me*. I'm not confused about fitness or nutrition. Trust *me*."

That was the beginning of a new kind of strength.

One concept in particular changed my life: macros. Instead of labeling foods as "good" or "bad," I learned to live in balance. Don taught me to start by hitting one gram of protein per pound of my preferred body weight. From there, I had flexibility with fats and carbs. If I was full but needed more energy, I'd add carbs. If I was hungry but close to my calorie cap, I'd add fats. There were no forbidden foods—just structure, strategy, and honesty. As long as I hit my protein and stayed under my calorie target, I was in the zone.

At first, I was overwhelmed. I thought carbs were the enemy. I thought fruit was evil because of the sugar. But Don patiently taught me that food wasn't the enemy—ignorance was. I didn't have to starve or suffer. I just had to learn.

I also began intermittent fasting—16 hours of fasting, 8 hours of eating. My last meal was around 9:00 PM, and I wouldn't eat again until after 1:00 PM the next day. It helped me stay focused and in control.

Here's what a typical day looked like:

- **First meal**: Unsweetened Greek yogurt with stevia, cinnamon, and berries

- **Restaurant breakfast (when dining out)**: Two over-easy eggs, a ham steak, and multigrain toast (no potatoes unless it was a treat day)

- **Lunch/Dinner**: Lean proteins like chicken breast or smoked fish with baked sweet potatoes or low-carb wraps

- **Evening snack**: Two protein shakes—one with 42g of protein, another with 30g

I averaged between 165–185 grams of protein per day. I tracked everything, planned ahead, and stayed one step ahead of my cravings. It wasn't always easy—but it became my new normal.

But let me be real—there were still hard days. One night, I ordered pizza out of stress and ate half of it before I could stop myself. I messaged Don in shame, expecting judgment.

He didn't text back—he *called* me. And instead of scolding, he laughed. Then he hit me with Scripture: "A righteous man falls seven times and rises again."

He said, "You got this. You're a winner. After everything you've been through, this is just a molehill. When you fall, you get back up. The only people who fail are the ones who quit. And you're not a quitter. You're a winner!"

That's when I learned to fail forward.

Still, the scale didn't always reflect the effort. Some weeks it went up. My heart would sink. But Don reminded me: This isn't about chasing a number. This is about building freedom. So we made a new rule: I would only weigh myself once a month. That one change liberated me from the tyranny of the number on the scale and allowed me to focus on consistency instead of quick results.

Because here's the truth:

Let's take it—together.

Journal Prompt

Do you already have an eating plan? What's working for you? What needs to change? Write about it here—honestly and without judgment.

Now go deeper:

- What emotional triggers affect your eating habits?
- Where do you need more support—spiritually, emotionally, physically?
- What are you willing to commit to today—not for perfection, but for progress?

THE BATTLE WITHIN
by Cynthia Mandel

CHAPTER 4: CHANGE STARTS FROM WITHIN

There are so many ways to get your steps in. But if you're just starting, take it slow. The goal isn't to go from zero to a marathon—it's to create momentum without burning yourself out.

At first, walking didn't feel like much. But it became everything. Because it wasn't just about steps. It was about learning how to show up for myself in a way I never had before.

For years, food had been my comfort, my coping mechanism, my escape. Movement? That was for other people. Athletes. Skinny people in cute gym clothes. Not me. But walking asked me to face myself—body, soul, and spirit—and to do it with kindness.

Exercise had never been part of my life, so naturally, it came with resistance. Not just from my muscles, but from my mind. I wasn't just battling sore legs—I was battling years of emotional weight, shame, and defeat. But with every step, something began to shift.

I started to see walking not as a punishment for my past, but as a declaration of healing. Each step wasn't just for my physical body—it was for my heart. My mind. My spirit.

Each step said: *You're not who you used to be.*

Each step said: *You're worth fighting for.*

I didn't walk on a treadmill, although plenty of people do. That's a great way to get in 20 minutes a day. But I preferred walking to and from the gym—1.75 miles each way. I even started looping around the gym between sets to rack up more steps.

I started small: 2,000 steps a day. Then I added 250 steps every other week. No pressure. Just slow, steady progress. That one strategy—gradual growth—changed everything.

In the past, I'd try to change everything at once. I'd go all-in, burn out fast, and end up discouraged. But this time, I did it differently. I celebrated every little victory. Whether it was 2,000 steps or 2,500, each one was a declaration: *I'm still in this.*

And it wasn't just a declaration to the world—it was one to myself.

You're not quitting this time. You're becoming.

Those small wins built the foundation for confidence. For the first time in a long time, I had proof that I could stick with something. That I was doing it. One step at a time.

Today, I aim for 8,000 to 10,000 steps a day. But if I fall short? No guilt. There's always tomorrow. Like eating well, this isn't a quick fix—it's a lifestyle. Just like brushing my teeth, walking has become part of my rhythm, my daily devotion to myself.

And being outside? That's healing all on its own. The fresh air clears my head. The quiet moments invite peace. Walking through the neighborhood or along a nature path grounds me. It's not just physical—it's spiritual. It's emotional. It's sacred.

For so long, my mind was filled with noise: past failures, shame, insecurity, pain. But when I walk, the rhythm of my steps becomes a kind of meditation. The negativity softens. The lies lose their grip. I begin to make space for something new: hope.

Yes, I walk in the rain, too. I grab an umbrella and throw on my older sneakers. I rotate my shoes so I don't wear the same pair two days in a row. Good sneakers matter—my favorites are Asics and Skechers because they're wider and more supportive. I wear lightweight workout clothes and keep it simple.

And while I walk? I feed my soul. I listen to sermons and podcasts. I fill my mind with the Word of God. I turn every walk into worship. It lifts me up and gets me aligned with truth before the day even begins.

Eventually, I started working out beyond walking. Don kept it simple: light weights, 10 reps, 2 sets, twice a week. I had no clue what any of it meant at first—but Don guided me every step of the way.

Here's what I learned:

- Start with a weight you can lift with effort—not struggle, just effort.
- "Reps" are the number of times you repeat the move; "sets" are how many rounds you do.
- Start with fewer reps if needed—just show up consistently.
- As you get stronger, increase reps and sets. Then, and only then, increase weight.

Don taught me to pair opposing muscle groups, like biceps and triceps, or chest and back. This allowed one group to rest while the other worked, maximizing results in less time. I loved it—quick, effective, and empowering.

And he drilled one golden rule into me: **Form over ego.**

Lifting heavy without proper form can injure your muscles, ligaments, or tendons. And injury? That'll sideline your progress fast.

So I pushed myself—but I did it smart. When my plan became too easy, I knew it was time to level up. And guess what? I started loving it. Not just the results—but the process.

I never thought I'd say that. But here I am.

Still, I get it—not everyone loves the gym. Some people live too far away, or they just don't vibe with that environment. That's okay. You can absolutely work out at home. All you need are a couple of hand weights—3s, 5s, 8s—maybe some resistance bands and a jump rope. I got mine online for cheap. No excuses.

Core work is essential, too. Your core keeps you balanced, upright, and stable. It's your body's foundation. And you can train it at home or in the gym.

Let's talk about cardio. It's great for your heart and endurance. Start where you are, then build. Aim for 10,000 steps if you can—but don't stress. What matters most is effort and consistency.

And don't underestimate the power of strength training. It builds muscle, boosts your metabolism, strengthens your bones, and floods your brain with endorphins. It doesn't take hours. Just 30–45 minutes can change your day—and your life.

I love working out in the morning. Why?

- It sets the tone for my day
- It lifts my mood
- And let's be honest—if I don't do it early, I probably won't do it at all

I use the Strange Sculpting App, which helps me log workouts, track progress, and communicate directly with Don. He customizes my plans and helps me make real-time adjustments. It's like having a coach in my pocket.

But even with all this effort, there were times when the scale didn't budge. I'd be working my tail off and lose... four pounds. Four! I'd be devastated.

And then Don would say something that stuck:

"Cynthia, a pound is a pound. But a pound of muscle takes up less space than a pound of fat."

Simple truth—but it changed everything.

Eventually, I stopped weighing myself altogether. Don reminded me that the scale doesn't define success—**your strength, stamina, and joy do.** And he was right.

We bumped up my workouts to four days a week. And in that first year with Don, I lost around 60 pounds.

But the biggest transformation? It wasn't just physical.

It was emotional. It was spiritual.

It was the belief that I was worth this effort.

Change doesn't start in the gym.

It starts in your heart.

It starts with a decision to show up for yourself every day. To make the next best choice.

To do what you can with what you've got. To honor your body as the temple it is.

You don't have to love working out. But I promise—if you give yourself a chance, you'll fall in love with how it makes you feel.

So take that first walk. Pick up those weights.

Press play on that podcast.

One small step at a time…

You're becoming stronger than you ever imagined.

Journal Prompt

Do you exercise regularly? Do you have a walking or workout routine? If not, what would you like to start doing?

Now dig deeper:

- What's held you back from moving your body in the past?
- What lie do you need to let go of to believe you're worth this effort?
- Write down a plan that feels realistic, encouraging, and doable—not perfect, just *possible*.

THE BATTLE WITHIN
by Cynthia Mandel

CHAPTER 5: SURVIVING AGAINST THE ODDS

A couple of years into my training journey with Don, everything came to a screeching halt.

I went into the hospital for a routine procedure—a surgery to repair a blockage caused by my gastric bypass, which I had done nearly twenty years earlier. It was supposed to be simple. I'd be in and out and back to my workouts in no time.

But what followed was anything but routine. I never saw it coming.

One moment, I was being prepped for surgery. The next, I was gone.

I slipped into septic shock. My organs began to fail. My blood pressure crashed. I was placed on a ventilator and spent the next fifteen days unconscious—suspended between life and death. My body lay motionless, but inside, everything was shutting down.

The doctors gave me less than a one percent chance of survival. They told my family to prepare for the worst.

They told my friends I wouldn't make it. They told the people who loved me to let go.

But God held on.

While machines kept my body alive, God kept my spirit. I didn't see Him. I didn't hear Him.

I didn't feel anything at all. I was just… gone.

It was like I had vanished from my own life—trapped in a silent body, locked in a place between here and eternity.

I wasn't fighting. I wasn't praying. I wasn't even aware. But God never left.

Even in the silence. Even when I couldn't whisper His name. Even when no one believed I'd wake up—**He stayed.**

THE BATTLE WITHIN
by Cynthia Mandel

And then, one day… I did wake up.

It wasn't peaceful. It wasn't cinematic.

There was no soft music or tearful reunion.

I woke up in a haze of confusion, panic, and pain. I couldn't move. I couldn't speak. My arms felt like cement. My legs were limp. My throat burned from the breathing tube. I tried to cry, but no tears came.

I was trapped in a body that no longer worked. And the fear hit me like a tidal wave.

Panic surged through my chest. The room spun. Machines beeped. Tubes ran from my arms, my nose, my mouth. Everything felt foreign. I had no idea what had happened. But deep in my gut, I knew: *something had gone terribly wrong.*

Everything I had worked for. Everything I had rebuilt— My strength. My health. My independence.

It all felt like it had been stolen from me in an instant.

My body was fragile. My mind was foggy. My soul felt shattered. But somewhere deep inside, I could still feel a flicker.

A whisper of strength.

A voice that said, *You're still here. Don't give up now.*

I had survived something most people don't.

But this wasn't just survival—it was resurrection.

God hadn't just pulled me through a health crisis.

He had pulled me back from the edge of death for a reason. He had whispered over my still body, "Not yet."

And that's when the real healing began. Recovery was slow. Painful. Humbling.

I had to relearn how to sit up, how to hold a fork, how to take a single step. My muscles had wasted away. My independence was gone.

THE BATTLE WITHIN
by Cynthia Mandel

I needed help for the most basic things— brushing my teeth, eating, even using the bathroom.

But each tiny milestone—each trembling motion, each deep breath, each whispered word—was a miracle.

God was rebuilding me, one moment at a time. Not just physically, but spiritually.

He was writing a new chapter on top of the one the enemy tried to erase.

Every struggle became sacred. Every breath was holy.

Every step forward was proof that **He wasn't finished with me yet.**

This wasn't just about regaining my strength. It was about trusting again.

Believing again. Living again.

Each day, I whispered prayers of thanks. Not polished prayers—just raw, broken ones. "Thank You for today."

"Help me get through this hour." "Don't let me give up."

And God met me in every one of them.

He didn't bring me through that valley just for me.

He brought me through it so I could tell *you* something:

Your story is not over.

I'm living proof that God can take what should've killed you—and use it to birth your purpose.

Today, I experience no lingering side effects. None.

Not a single one.

My doctors are amazed. They have no explanation. But I do: **Jesus.**

He resurrected me from death—not just so I could walk again, but so I could *run* with purpose.

So I could help others become whole.

So I could point to the Healer who didn't just restore my body—but renewed my mind, revived my heart, and redeemed my entire life.

Now, I walk in purpose.

I'm more passionate than ever about helping others rise—not just to lose weight, but to break free. Not just to build muscle, but to build *hope*.

If you're reading this, wondering if you can come back from your darkest valley— You can.

I've been there. I've almost died.

I've been too broken to speak.

I've felt the weight of regret and the sting of starting over. But grace found me.

And it can find you, too.

Your pain doesn't disqualify you. Your past doesn't define you. You're still breathing? Then God's still working.

He's not done with you yet.

There's more to this story, and I'll share it in my next book, *The Girl That Nobody Wanted*. That book will walk you through the long road from total abandonment to radical acceptance.

But let me leave you with this:

You are not forgotten. You are not forsaken. You are not finished.

Journal Prompt

What obstacles have you had to overcome in your life? Write them down. Big or small—name them.

Now take it deeper:

- What did each challenge *teach* you?
- Where did you see God move—even if it took time to recognize it?
- Are there any parts of your story you thought disqualified you? Write them here— and remind yourself: *God can use even this.*

Don't edit. Don't filter. Just be real. Your healing starts with honesty.

_____
_____
_____
_____
_____
_____
_____
_____
_____
_____
_____
_____
_____

THE BATTLE WITHIN
by Cynthia Mandel

CHAPTER 6:
IDENTIFYING EMOTIONAL TRIGGERS

First things first—what exactly is a trigger?

A trigger is any event, comment, feeling, or situation that stirs up emotional discomfort, often rooted in past pain. It might be something small, like a tone of voice, or something bigger, like rejection or loss.

For me, that discomfort almost always sent me straight to the refrigerator.

Food wasn't just something I ate when I was hungry—it was my comfort, my shield, my escape route.

From early childhood, after my father abandoned me, and through years of emotional neglect and abuse, food became the one constant.

It never judged me. Never left me.

Never hurt me.

But it also never healed me.

The real problem? I didn't understand what was driving me to eat. I had never been taught how to process my emotions. So I shoved them down—bite by bite.

Sad? Eat. Angry? Eat. Rejected? Eat. Ashamed? Eat.

It gave me a moment of peace... but the pain always came back stronger. This became my cycle:

Emotional trigger → Emotional eating → Emotional numbness → Emotional regret.

Over time, I became disconnected from my own feelings. I wasn't healing—I was hiding.

I was reacting, not responding.

What Triggers You?

Triggers come in many forms. Some are loud and obvious. Others sneak in, dressed up like normal moments.

Here are some of mine:

- Anxiety
- Fear
- Abandonment
- Anger
- Being ignored or dismissed
- Criticism or judgment
- Sadness
- Abuse
- Grief
- Helplessness
- Someone trying to control me
- Rejection
- Loneliness
- Authority figures
- Being undervalued

Sound familiar?

Here's what I've learned:

Your triggers are not weaknesses.

They're signals.

They're pointing to wounds that haven't fully healed yet. The key to overcoming them is learning to:

1. Identify what your triggers are
2. Recognize how they affect you
3. Respond to them with truth—not with old habits

Most triggers stem from trauma. And trauma doesn't have to be dramatic to be damaging. A comment. A look. A memory. Even being left out—especially if it echoes something painful from childhood—can feel like a deep cut.

THE BATTLE WITHIN
by Cynthia Mandel

The Day My Trigger Was Pulled

Not long ago, I was talking with a group of people, and one of the men looked at me and said, "Wow, if you get any thinner, you're going to have every man chasing after you!"

He probably thought it was a compliment.

But to me? It was a full-blown emotional landmine.

In an instant, I felt fear, panic, and the familiar urge to disappear. His comment yanked me right back to the terrified little girl who had been violated and silenced.

What most people didn't understand was that the 430 pounds I carried weren't just physical. They were armor.

If I could make myself invisible or undesirable, maybe I could protect myself. Maybe no one would ever look at me *that way* again.

So when he said that, it wasn't about him. It was about *then*.

It was about the trauma that still lingered beneath the surface.

I excused myself, stepped outside, and sat in my car. My heart was racing. My body was tense. My first instinct was to numb out. I thought of drive-thrus, snacks, comfort food. But then I took a deep breath and prayed:

"This isn't your story anymore." "You are in control now."

"God is here. You are safe."

And in that moment, for the first time, I didn't run. I didn't eat.

I stayed.

I breathed.

And I *healed*—even just a little more.

THE BATTLE WITHIN
by Cynthia Mandel

Breaking the Silence

Since I was molested at six and gang-raped at fourteen (more on that in *The Girl That Nobody Wanted*), I learned to hide—not just physically, but emotionally. I wore the weight as protection, thinking it could keep me safe.

Let's be honest—**it didn't.**

But in my mind, it gave me distance. That day in the car, I prayed again:

"Father, I know this fear is not from You. In Jesus' name, I release this old story. I reject this lie. I accept Your truth. I am safe. I am whole. I am Yours."

And little by little… the fear lifted.

Healing isn't a light switch. It's a process.

But every time you choose truth over reaction, you take back your power.

Food: The Most Accepted Drug

Food is everywhere—at weddings, funerals, birthdays, breakups. We eat when we celebrate. We eat when we grieve.

And like any drug, food can be used to *numb* what we don't want to feel. It was never about hunger.

It was about *not feeling*.

But food never solved the problem. It only buried it deeper.

And every time I ate to escape, I only added shame on top of pain.

How I Started to Break the Cycle

Real change didn't begin when I stopped eating emotionally. It began when I started **facing my pain head-on.**

Now, when I feel triggered, I *pause*. I pray.

I journal.

I take a walk.

I breathe through it.

I don't do it perfectly, but I do it intentionally.

And each time I resist the old urge, I grow stronger.

Tips for Handling Triggers

- **Name the trigger.** Give it language. That robs it of power.
- **Create space.** Step away, take a breath, go for a walk.
- **Notice physical symptoms.** Clenched jaw, tight chest, racing thoughts—pay attention.
- **Ask yourself:** What am I *really* feeling? What's underneath this?
- **Don't resist the emotion**— invite it, feel it, and release it.
- **Plan for next time.** What tool will you use—prayer, journaling, movement?

Because here's the truth:

You can feel it and survive it.

You don't need to eat it away.

You don't need to hide from it.

Every time you feel the feeling, deal with it, and move on—you break the chain.

ꞓ *Triggers & Truths Exercise*

Write down the triggers that set you off—and how you can respond with strength instead of shame.

Emotional Trigger	Grounded Response / Truth
Feeling rejected	I am accepted by God and don't need to earn love.

Emotional Trigger	Grounded Response / Truth
Harsh criticism	I can grow without agreeing with every opinion.
Feeling out of control	I can pause, breathe, and choose my next best step.
Loneliness	I am never truly alone—God is with me always.

Again, encourage personal reflection:

"Use this chart to start replacing old reactions with truth. The goal isn't perfection—it's awareness."

_____
_____
_____
_____
_____
_____
_____
_____
_____
_____

The Trauma Cycle

This loop is especially brutal for those of us who've experienced deep wounds:

Trigger → Foggy thinking → Emotional reaction → Guilt → Repeat

Whether your escape is food, alcohol, shopping, sex, scrolling, or overworking—it doesn't heal the pain. It just hides it.

But facing it? That's where the freedom is.

Ask Yourself…

- Where do your triggers come from?
- Who hurt you?
- What moment shaped your fears?
- What lie have you believed about yourself because of it?

For me, my deep sense of worthlessness began when my father left. And it was reinforced by years spent in institutions where I felt invisible and unwanted.

I used to believe I was less than dirt. But that was a lie.

And lies lose their power the moment we drag them into the light.

Journal Prompt

Can you identify any emotional or physical triggers in your life? Go deeper:

- What lie have you believed about yourself because of them?
- What might God be trying to show you through your reactions?
- How can you respond with grace, instead of retreating into old patterns? Don't rush this. Don't filter. This is your healing space.

THE BATTLE WITHIN
by Cynthia Mandel

CHAPTER 7:
REWRITING THE STORY: OVERCOMING LIMITING BELIEFS

What are limiting beliefs?

Limiting beliefs are mindsets that prevent us from becoming who God created us to be. They're negative thoughts that act as invisible barriers, stopping us from pursuing our dreams and fulfilling our true potential.

For much of my life, I didn't realize that my internal beliefs were working against me. I had absorbed so many painful messages from childhood—born from abandonment, neglect, abuse, and heartbreak. These weren't truths. They were lies formed by wounds that never got a chance to heal. I believed I was unlovable, incapable of change, and destined to fail. These weren't just occasional thoughts; they were the lens through which I viewed my life, my future, and my worth.

These beliefs weren't facts—they were survival stories. I created them to protect myself from more pain. But in reality, they kept me stuck in cycles of fear, shame, and self-sabotage. Every time I said, "I can't," or "I'm not good enough," I was reinforcing a false narrative. And as long as I clung to those beliefs, I could never step into freedom.

What Limiting Beliefs Sound Like

Limiting beliefs usually take root in childhood. They're shaped by how we were treated, what we were told, and how we internalized the hard moments in our lives. Here are a few of mine:

- No one likes me.
- I'm not worthy of being loved.
- I'm not good enough or smart enough.
- I'm too fat / too old / too short / too young.
- This is just the way I am—I can't change.
- I'll fail, so why even try?
- Everything bad that happens is my fault.

Maybe yours sound different, but if you listen closely, you'll hear the same lies in your own head. They may whisper that you're too late, too broken, too far gone, or too undeserving. But those lies don't define you—they confine you.

Our brains often create these beliefs to protect us. But instead of guarding us, they imprison us. My brain, trying to keep me safe from disappointment, fed me lies to keep me in my comfort zone—even if that zone was full of dysfunction.

For years, I tried to grow and improve—working out, dieting, striving to be "better." But it felt like running in place. Why? Because I was still tethered to emotional baggage. It's like trying to fly a plane with a 500-pound boulder strapped to the tail. No amount of effort will lift you off the ground until you cut it loose.

How to Overcome Limiting Beliefs

Here's what I learned about overcoming limiting beliefs:

- Identify the belief.
- Acknowledge that it's just a belief—not reality.
- Challenge it.
- Replace it with a new, empowering belief.
- Affirm the new belief consistently.
- Ask: Where is this coming from? Is it true?

The Truth About Change

I never spent years dieting, working out, trying harder—but I always ended up back at square one. I believed I was so overweight that why bother it would never happen.

Why?

Because I hadn't dealt with the emotional weight holding me back. The battle wasn't just in my body.

It was in my mind.

Real change began when I learned to:

- Identify the limiting belief

- Recognize it's a belief—not a fact
- Challenge it
- Replace it with truth
- Repeat the new truth until I believed it

A Belief That Nearly Broke Me

One of the biggest lies I carried was:

"I'm not worthy of love."

That one belief shaped everything. It dictated how I saw myself, how I treated my body, and how I let people treat me.

I believed love had to be earned. That I had to be perfect to deserve it. So I built walls. I pushed people away. And when they left, I told myself, "See? I knew they would."

It became a self-fulfilling prophecy. Then one day, a still small voice inside asked:

"What if this isn't true?"

And I had a breakthrough:

If I keep believing I'm unlovable, I'll never let real love in—even when it's right in front of me.

So, I flipped the script. I started affirming:

"I am lovable just as I am."

"I am worthy of love, and I am open to receiving it."

At first, it felt like I was lying to myself. But I kept saying it. Kept writing it. Kept breathing it in. And eventually... I started to believe it.

Things began to shift. I stopped expecting abandonment. I stopped sabotaging relationships. I stopped hiding behind food and shame. I started living.

Fully.

Freely.

Finally.

My Weight Was Never the Real Problem

It took me years to realize I wasn't overeating because I loved food. I was overeating because I was avoiding pain.

My size became my shield. I believed that if I stayed invisible, I'd be safe. But safety built on fear is still a prison.

Once I confronted the beliefs behind the behavior, everything began to change. I shifted from:

"I'll never lose this weight." to

"I am worth the effort to heal."

That one shift changed everything. And here's the part no one tells you—it wasn't as hard as I thought it would be. Once my mind aligned with truth, my body followed.

You can rewrite your story too. It doesn't start with a diet. It starts with a decision.

One thought.

One truth.

My Personal Breakthrough

For years, I lived under the belief: "I'm not worthy to be loved." It shaped my relationships, my self-image, and my choices. I believed love had to be earned—that I had to be perfect to deserve it. So I pushed people away. I expected abandonment, and then subconsciously created it.

One day, I had a breakthrough: If I believed I wasn't lovable, I would never let love in—even if it was right in front of me. I made a conscious choice to flip the script. I started affirming: "I am lovable just as I am. I am worthy of love, and I am open to receiving it." At first, I didn't fully believe it. But over time, it started to sink in.

This shift changed everything. I stopped sabotaging love. I stopped expecting rejection. I redefined love—not as a reward, but as something I was born worthy of.

Before I rewrote this belief, I never accepted someone saying, "I love you." My inner voice would scream, "No, you don't!" or "You'll leave, just like everyone else." That belief even affected my health. Part of the reason I stayed overweight was because I thought my size protected me. It was a shield—a wall I built around my heart. When pain hit, I ate to numb it. But that wall wasn't keeping me safe. It was keeping me trapped.

The truth? My weight was never the real problem. My beliefs were. Once I faced them, challenged them, and replaced them, everything began to change. I started letting people in. I embraced vulnerability. I stopped hiding behind food and began living with intention.

When I shifted from "I'll never lose this weight" to "I am worth the effort to heal and grow," everything changed. And you know what? It wasn't nearly as hard as I thought—once I got my mind in alignment with the truth.

Your Turn to Rewrite the Story

You can rewrite your story too. It begins with one thought, one truth, one brave decision to believe something different. Let this be the chapter where your new story begins.

Journal Prompt:

Reflect on the limiting beliefs that have shaped your life.

- What limiting belief has held me back the most in my life?
- Where did this belief come from—was it spoken over me, or did I create it from pain?
- Is this belief actually true? What evidence do I have that proves otherwise?
- What empowering truth can I replace it with today?
- How can I affirm this new belief daily until it becomes my reality?

THE BATTLE WITHIN
by Cynthia Mandel

CHAPTER 8:
SPOTLIGHT: DON STRANGE — THE TRAINER BEHIND THE REAL CHANGE

Don's journey in fitness started at 23, but it wasn't a straight climb to the top. He's been lean, he's been overweight, and he's fought his way back more than once. That's why he trains without judgment — because he's lived every phase himself.

His philosophy is simple: *Discipline Builds Destiny*. Show up when it's hard. Stay consistent when motivation fades. Treat your body like it matters — because it does.

Don doesn't chase scale numbers. He builds bodies through recomposition — more muscle, less fat — because muscle takes up less space and changes how you feel in your skin.

I'm living proof of his work: over 150 pounds gone after 60, stronger now than I was in my 40s. Behind the scenes, Don calculates my macros, designs my workouts, and tracks it all through the Strange Sculpting App. I'm the coach in your corner, but he's the architect making it possible. Together, we've built not just a program — but a way of life.

Helping Women Take the Reins

Cynthia's not just a client—she's a force.

She didn't start perfect. She started consistent. Now she's coaching other women through the same process—with my systems behind the scenes.

Most women think they need a complete overhaul. They don't. They need a clear path, and the guts to take the first step. That's what we give them: a plan, a process, and a partnership that doesn't quit when things get hard.

My Philosophy: Discipline Builds Destiny

I teach one core truth:

If you can't control your body, your life's running you—not the other way around.

- Show up when it sucks.
- Be consistent when motivation dies.
- Treat your body like it matters—because it does.

We train for recomposition—more muscle, less fat. The scale might lie, but your clothes won't. Transformation starts with what you do when no one claps.

What Working With Us Looks Like

Cynthia is the coach in your corner.

I'm behind the curtain—building the blueprint.

- Your plan? Custom.
- Your macros? Calculated.
- Your workouts? Designed for results.

And it's all delivered through the Strange Sculpting App no guesswork, no fluff.

This isn't some Pinterest workout plan.

It's a mission—with teeth.

Let this be the first day of your new story.

Helping Women Rewrite Their Stories Through Fitness

Cynthia is living proof that it's never too late to begin again.

She's over 60. She's lost more than 150 pounds. And more than that—she's transformed her *life*, not just her body.

Many women feel overwhelmed by the idea of starting. But you don't need perfection. You just need **progress**.

That's what I help deliver: not just a program, but a path. A way to show up, even when it's hard.

My mission is to equip women with tools, knowledge, and

encouragement—to help them feel strong, capable, and confident in their own skin.

My Philosophy: Discipline Builds Destiny

I teach my clients that discipline in fitness mirrors discipline in life.

- Show up when it's hard.
- Choose consistency over intensity.
- Honor the temple God gave you.

Every workout, every meal, every rest day—it's all an act of worship and self-respect. We also focus on body composition—not just the number on the scale.

Muscle weighs more than fat, but takes up less space. So even if the scale stalls, your body is still transforming.

That's called **recomposition**, and it's a big focus in the early stages of training.

Working with Cynthia (and Me)

Cynthia is your coach—but I'm right behind the scenes.

I help build your custom plan. I consult on your macros. I design your workouts. Together, we use the **Strange Sculpting App** to deliver everything right to your phone.

This isn't just a fitness program.

It's a personalized, faith-fueled **partnership**.

You'll be supported. Seen. Stretched. And celebrated.

Journal Prompt:

Think about a time in your life when discipline—not motivation—kept you moving forward.

- Describe a goal you once set (fitness-related or not) and the obstacles you faced along the way.
- How did showing up consistently, even when you didn't feel like it, change your outcome?
- Write down one area of your life right now where you could apply the "Discipline Builds Destiny" mindset.
- What small, repeatable action could you commit to daily that would move you closer to your goal?

_____
_____
_____
_____
_____
_____
_____
_____
_____
_____
_____
_____
_____
_____
_____

THE BATTLE WITHIN
by Cynthia Mandel

CHAPTER 9:
LIVING IN THE FREEDOM YOU FOUGHT FOR

Turning the Breakthrough into a Lifestyle

Breakthrough is powerful.

But if you stop there, you'll eventually slide back into what broke you.

Freedom doesn't come from a single moment of clarity—it comes from a daily decision to live like the chains are already broken.

So let's talk about what happens **after** the miracle. After the weight comes off.

After you've confronted the pain, dismantled the lies, and stared down the parts of you that you never thought could change.

The fight may be over, but now you've got to learn how to *live free.*

Freedom Isn't a Finish Line—It's a Way of Life

I used to believe freedom was something I'd eventually *arrive* at—like once I hit my goal weight, healed my trauma, or stopped emotional eating, I'd be "done." A finish line. Cue the confetti.

But here's what I learned:

Freedom isn't the end. It's the beginning.

Living in freedom requires just as much intentionality as fighting for it.

Because if you're not careful, old patterns will sneak back in—disguised as comfort, survival, or even *normal.*

The version of me that used to binge eat, hide, and self-sabotage didn't vanish overnight. She still tries to show up sometimes. Yes even now, that's why you have to renew your mind each day,

But now?

I know how to deal with her—with love, with truth, and with a clear **no thank you**.

You're Not That Girl Anymore

After I started healing, losing weight, and changing my life, a strange fear crept in:

Who am I now that I'm not broken?

For years, I wore pain like a second skin. Trauma shaped how I moved, how I spoke, how I dressed—even how I breathed.

When the healing took root, I had to meet myself again—without the weight and without the wounds.

And I'll be honest: it was uncomfortable.

The "old me" tried to stage a comeback: over and over again even to this day. "See? I knew it wouldn't last."

"They don't really mean that compliment." "Stay small—it's safer there."

But I refused to let her have the mic anymore. As soon as she starts I counter with: I'm not that girl.

I'm not that story.

I'm not the shame I carried.

I'm the woman who survived her. I'm the woman who rewrote her.

And so are you.

From Recovery to Rhythm

Here's the truth no one talks about:

Breakthrough is exhausting.

Healing takes work.

Breaking generational cycles is emotional labor.

Losing 253 pounds—physically and emotionally—is no small feat.

So once the dust settles, you need rhythms in place that help you maintain your progress **without burning out**. For me, that looks like:

- Meal planning—with grace, not perfection
- Working out because I love my body, not because I hate it
- Daily time with God—journaling, praying, refueling
- Getting outside for walks to reset my soul
- Letting myself rest without guilt It's not about being "on" all the time.

It's about being consistent with what gives you life.

Slip-Ups Are Not Setbacks

Yes, I have days where I eat off plan.

Yes, I have days where motivation takes a vacation.

But here's the difference: I don't throw the whole thing away.

When you're living in freedom, one mistake isn't an excuse to self-destruct. You *breathe.*

You *adjust.*

You *keep going.*

You've already proven you can fight for your life.

Now prove that you can *sustain* your healing—without punishing yourself for being human.

Protecting Your Freedom

Just because you're healed doesn't mean you're immune.

Freedom needs to be protected.

That means:

- Setting boundaries with people who trigger old pain
- Noticing your patterns when you're stressed, tired, or feeling unworthy
- Staying connected to God, your coach, mentor

Journal Prompt:

Reflect on how you can turn a personal breakthrough into a lasting lifestyle.

- Describe a breakthrough moment you've experienced—big or small. What changed in your mindset or life after it?
- What old patterns or "old you" behaviors still try to sneak back in? How do you recognize them when they show up?
- Write down three daily rhythms or habits you could commit to that would help you protect your progress and live in freedom.
- How can you respond with love and truth when your old self tries to take over again?

THE BATTLE WITHIN
by Cynthia Mandel

CHAPTER 10 : YOUR NEXT S.T.E.P.

Stepping Out, Stepping Up, and Stepping Into Freedom

- You didn't just read a book.

You've walked through years of emotional pain, physical battles, and spiritual warfare—and *you're still standing.*

Stronger. Smarter. Freer.

But this? This is just the beginning.
Because the real question now is:

What's your next S.T.E.P.?

Transformation isn't a one-time event. It's a lifestyle.
And now—it's time to live in the freedom you fought so hard to find.

N.E.X.T. — The Future You're Walking Into

N – Never Go Back
You've come too far to entertain old habits, toxic voices, or small thinking.
When the enemy tries to drag you back into who you used to be, remind him:
"That girl doesn't live here anymore."

E – Elevate Your Environment
Surround yourself with people who speak life, not death.
Build a circle that calls you higher—not back.
Set boundaries with those who drain your energy, and lean into the community that fuels your faith.

X – Exchange Lies for Truth
Start paying attention to your inner dialogue. When a lie shows up—

"I'll always struggle."
"I'm too old."
"I'm not enough…"

Replace it with what God says about you.
Lie: "I can't do this."
Truth: "I can do all things through Christ who strengthens me." — *Philippians 4:13*

T – Take Territory
You didn't go through all this healing just to play small.
It's time to step into the fullness of who you are.

That business idea?
That speaking opportunity?
That ministry dream?
GO AFTER IT.

"Every place where you set your foot will be yours." — *Deuteronomy 11:24*

S.T.E.P. — The Freedom You're Meant to Live

S – Surrender Your Past
Before you can rise, you have to release.
Let go of what hurt you. Lay it at the feet of Jesus.
You don't need to carry shame, regret, or guilt another day.

"Forget the former things; do not dwell on the past." — *Isaiah 43:18*

THE BATTLE WITHIN
by Cynthia Mandel

T – Trust the Process
Healing takes time.
Progress isn't always visible, but it's always happening.
Trust that every act of obedience—every healthy choice, every prayer, every walk—is making you stronger.

E – Embrace Your Identity

You are no longer *"the girl who messed up."*
You are a daughter of the King.
Chosen. Loved. Redeemed.

Walk in that truth.
Own it. Speak it.

P – Pursue Healing With Purpose

This is more than a weight loss story.
This is a redemption story.

Pursue wholeness in every area—**mind, body, and soul**.
And remember: you're not just doing this for you.
You're doing it for the women watching you rise.

A Final Word from Cynthia

You've just walked with me through **The Battle Within**.
And I pray that somewhere in these pages, you heard something that whispered:

"You are not alone."
"You are not stuck."
"You are not finished."

Maybe your battle has been food.
Maybe it's shame.

Maybe it's trauma, heartbreak, or the haunting echo of abandonment.

Whatever it is—you've taken the first steps toward a new life. Now it's time to keep walking.

If you want to go deeper into my story—into the **childhood that shaped me**, the **trauma that nearly destroyed me**, and the **God who never let me go**—
my next book, **The Girl That Nobody Wanted**, is where we go there together.

But for today, let me leave you with this:

You are already becoming the woman God always saw in you.

Keep stepping.
Keep rising.
Keep choosing freedom.

Because your next step?

It's the one that changes everything.

THE BATTLE WITHIN
by Cynthia Mandel

Declaration

I am not who I used to be.
I am strong. I am free. I am loved.
And I am just getting started.

I take the next step with boldness—knowing that:
My healing has purpose.
My future has hope.

And Your Community

Recognize when you're slipping—and course-correct with grace.
You didn't come this far just to let a toxic person, a bad day, or a number on the scale steal your peace.

Your freedom is sacred.

Guard it like it is.

Discipline Is a Form of Self-Love

Discipline used to feel like punishment. Like something I *had* to do because I wasn't enough.

Now I see it for what it really is:

A gift.

Discipline is how I love myself enough to follow through. When I make a healthy meal...

When I get in my steps...

When I resist the old urge to numb out with food...

...I'm telling myself:

"You're worth showing up for."

It's not about restriction. It's about *respect*.

Becoming the Leader You Needed

Here's the full-circle moment:

The healed version of you becomes hope for someone else.

You don't have to be perfect to lead. You don't need a stage or a platform.

You just need a story—and the courage to tell it.

Every time I shared my pain, my healing, or my tools, it reminded me just how far I'd come. It kept me grounded.

It kept me grateful.

Your story is the key that could unlock someone else's prison.

So don't wait until you "arrive."

You're already equipped with what someone else needs.

This Is Your New Normal

You've done the hard work. Now it's time to *live in the result*.

Not chasing perfection. Not looking back.

Just *owning* the freedom God gave you.

Every morning, remind yourself:

"I don't live in bondage anymore."

"I don't make decisions from trauma anymore." "I walk in truth, peace, health, and strength." "I'm not just surviving—I'm *thriving*."

You've Rewritten the Story—Now Walk in It

This is your life now.

Not the one you escaped from—the one you *created*.

You are no longer defined by what hurt you. You are defined by the fact that you healed.

So walk with your head high. Speak with confidence.

Take up space. Set boundaries. Fuel your body. Guard your peace. Love your life.

Because this freedom?

You fought for it.

Now go live like it's yours.

Journal Prompt

What rhythms and boundaries do you need in place to protect your freedom? Now, go further:

- Write a declaration of who you are now.
- What lies have you left behind—and what truth are you walking in today?
- How does freedom feel—and how will you guard it, daily? Let this become your new anthem.
- What part of my old story am I ready to surrender today?
- What lie have I believed about myself that I now reject?
- What truth will I speak over myself daily?
- What bold step can I take this week toward living in my healing?

_____

_____

_____

_____

_____

_____

_____

_____

_____

THE BATTLE WITHIN
by Cynthia Mandel

DON'S TRAINING PHILOSOPHY

1. What you put into your mind is even more important than what you put into your body.
2. What you do *consistently* matters more than what you do *occasionally*.
3. Your lifestyle and habits shape your future far more than your genetics.

"The mind can achieve what it can conceive and believe." — Don Strange

Reflection Prompt

What fitness goals would you like to accomplish?

Write them here—and be bold. Then list the *small steps* you can take this week to start sculpting the life and body you deserve.

THE BATTLE WITHIN
by Cynthia Mandel

THE BATTLE WITHIN
by Cynthia Mandel

www.ingramcontent.com/pod-product-compliance
Lightning Source LLC
Chambersburg PA
CBHW061804070526
44586CB00023B/2704